APRIL 2016

The European Union in a Reconnecting Eurasia

Foreign Economic and Security Interests

AUTHOR
Marlene Laruelle

EDITOR
Jeffrey Mankoff

Eurasia from the Outside In

A REPORT OF THE
CSIS RUSSIA AND EURASIA PROGRAM

CSIS | CENTER FOR STRATEGIC &
INTERNATIONAL STUDIES

ROWMAN &
LITTLEFIELD
Lanham • Boulder • New York • London

About CSIS

For over 50 years, the Center for Strategic and International Studies (CSIS) has worked to develop solutions to the world's greatest policy challenges. Today, CSIS scholars are providing strategic insights and bipartisan policy solutions to help decisionmakers chart a course toward a better world.

CSIS is a nonprofit organization headquartered in Washington, D.C. The Center's 220 full-time staff and large network of affiliated scholars conduct research and analysis and develop policy initiatives that look into the future and anticipate change.

Founded at the height of the Cold War by David M. Abshire and Admiral Arleigh Burke, CSIS was dedicated to finding ways to sustain American prominence and prosperity as a force for good in the world. Since 1962, CSIS has become one of the world's preeminent international institutions focused on defense and security; regional stability; and transnational challenges ranging from energy and climate to global health and economic integration.

Thomas J. Pritzker was named chairman of the CSIS Board of Trustees in November 2015. Former U.S. deputy secretary of defense John J. Hamre has served as the Center's president and chief executive officer since 2000.

CSIS does not take specific policy positions; accordingly, all views expressed herein should be understood to be solely those of the author(s).

ISBN: 978-1-4422-5932-4 (pb); 978-1-4422-5933-1 (eBook)

Center for Strategic & International Studies
1616 Rhode Island Avenue, NW
Washington, DC 20036
202-887-0200 | www.csis.org

Rowman & Littlefield
4501 Forbes Boulevard
Lanham, MD 20706
301-459-3366 | www.rowman.com

Contents

Preface

In January 2014, the CSIS Russia and Eurasia Program launched its Eurasia Initiative. The vast Eurasian landmass, stretching from China in the east to Europe in the west and from the Arctic Ocean in the north to the Indian Ocean in the south, includes some of the world's most powerful and dynamic states, as well as some of the world's most intractable challenges. Scholars and analysts are accustomed to focusing separately on Eurasia's various regions—Europe, the former Soviet Union, East Asia, South Asia, and Southeast Asia—rather than on the interactions between them. The goal of this initiative is to focus on these interactions, while analyzing and understanding Eurasia in a comprehensive way.

Today, more than any time since the collapse of the Silk Road five centuries ago, understanding these individual regions is impossible without also understanding the connections between them. Over the past two decades, Eurasia has begun to slowly reconnect, with the emergence of new trade relationships and transit infrastructures, as well as the integration of Russia, China, and India into the global economy. Even as this reconnection is under way, the center of economic dynamism in Eurasia, and in the world as a whole, continues shifting to the East. The impact of these shifts is potentially enormous, but they remain poorly understood because of intellectual and bureaucratic stovepiping in government and the broader analytic community.

Following its twin report series on Central Asia and on the South Caucasus, respectively, the CSIS Russia and Eurasia Program is now releasing papers in a third series we are informally calling "Eurasia from the Outside In." If the first two Eurasia Initiative report series focused on how economic connectivity and shifting political alignments looked from the interior of Eurasia, the current series focuses on the perspectives of the large, powerful countries that make up the periphery of the Eurasian landmass, namely China, India, Iran, Russia, and Turkey, as well as the European Union. The six reports in this series, each written by a leading local scholar of Eurasia, seek to provide insight into where Eurasia fits among the foreign economic and security priorities of these major powers.

While the most visible components of Eurasia's reconnection are infrastructure projects, the longer term result has been a reshuffling of relations between the post-Soviet states of Central

Asia and the South Caucasus on the one hand, and the major regional powers on the other. When the states of Central Asia and the South Caucasus became independent 25 years ago, they were closely tied to Russia. Over the past two and a half decades, they have developed a complex web of linkages to the other Eurasian powers, who themselves have devoted increased resources and attention to Eurasia in the years since the Soviet collapse. Russia still remains the dominant security provider in Central Asia and most of the South Caucasus. However China, the European Union, India, Iran, and Turkey all play major, if still evolving, roles in the region as well.

The scholars we have commissioned to write these reports bring a deep knowledge of their respective countries as well as a strong understanding of developments across Eurasia. While they are addressing a common set of questions, their answers and perspectives often diverge. Our goal is not consensus. Rather, it is to provide the best possible analysis of the roles these states are playing in shaping Eurasia's reconnection. We chose to seek out scholars from the countries being studied so that these reports would not be U.S.-centric, but would rather throw light on how Ankara, Beijing, Brussels, Moscow, New Delhi, and Tehran conceive of their respective interests and strategies in Eurasia.

With this report series, and indeed with the Eurasia Initiative more generally, we hope to encourage analysts and policymakers to think about Eurasia in a holistic way. Eurasia is much more than just the periphery of the old Soviet Union: it is a patchwork of states and peoples whose relationships are shifting rapidly. It is Central Asia, but it is also Europe; the South Caucasus but also India. Most importantly, it is the connections that are emerging and developing between these various states and regions. Our "Eurasia from the Inside Out" report series highlights the extent to which the comparatively small states at Eurasia's center have become a focal point for the economic and political engagement of the much larger powers surrounding them, and hence why these states continue to matter for global peace and prosperity.

Acknowledgments

I would like to thank Jos Boonstra for reading a draft of this report and for his advice. All mistakes remain mine.

This report is made possible by the generous support of the Smith Richardson Foundation, the Carnegie Corporation of New York, the Ministry of Foreign Affairs of the Republic of Kazakhstan, and Carlos Bulgheroni. We are also extremely grateful for program support provided by the Carnegie Corporation of New York to the CSIS Russia and Eurasia Program.

The View from Brussels

With its multiplicity of voices and institutions, the European Union is a complex political entity. Among its institutions, the European Commission (which represents unified European institutions) offers one voice, the European Council (which represents the member states) a second—although it is often close to the first—and the Parliament (which represents European citizens) a third—one that differs with the previous two both on domestic and on external policies. Europe's interests are also transmitted through transatlantic institutions such as NATO or the Organization for Security and Co-operation in Europe (OSCE), which have their own agendas, and thus both strengthen and complicate the European presence in the Eurasian region. Last but not least, member states, particularly the most powerful, have their own voices, narratives, and strategy. This diversity of views from Europe has expanded drastically in recent years: divergent energy strategies among member states and then the Greek crisis and the migrant emergency situation have worked to blur the unity of EU discourse, and voices of disagreement have drowned out those of unity. Today, on many of the major international questions of concern to the European Union, cacophony prevails, including in relation to the post-Soviet states of the South Caucasus and Central Asia.

In their administrative schemas, EU institutions and member states continue to regard the post-Soviet region (apart from the three Baltic states that have joined the European Union) as a common geographic space that remains—willingly or not—under Moscow's influence.

Europe's historical links with the region are varied and can be divided into five categories. The Baltic countries have always been considered as belonging to Europe, as they were the only ones among the 15 post-Soviet republics to have formed independent states in the interwar period, though they were under Russian domination throughout the nineteenth century. A second category comprises Ukraine, Belarus, and Moldova, which have been historically divided between European empires and the Russian realm. The three states of the South Caucasus have never been part of any historical European entity and are remote geographically—unless Turkey is regarded as an integral part of Europe. Yet as two of them, Armenia and Georgia, are Christian, and as the Armenian diaspora is influential, in particular in France, and as Georgia has always shown a strong pro-Western attitude, both are perceived as pro-European.[1] The fourth group is made up of the five countries of Central Asia, which from Europe's perspective are the most remote, both geographically and in terms of cultural influence.

The fifth category comprises Russia alone. The question of the Europe-Russia relationship over time is complex. Russia has been a European power from its foundation. It has participated in European diplomatic relations since the Middle Ages, and fully integrated into the European diplomatic arena during the reign of Peter the Great in the late seventeenth and early eighteenth centuries. It has participated in many intra-European alliances, from the Grand Alliance against Napoleon to the Triple Entente. Europe is, however, divided over the question of Russia's place, and here two heritages clash. The stakes are above all about memory. Western Europe largely continues to identify the USSR as one of the major victors of World War II, thanks to the enormous efforts and sacrifices Moscow made in the struggle against nazism. In this version of the past, the Iron Curtain that followed World War II was a sad consequence of the war that should be relegated to history. The countries of central and Eastern Europe that were part of the socialist camp from 1945 to 1989 very often promote a different view, one in which the Soviet Union and Nazi Germany are essentially equal in their lust for conquest and domination. This historical framework is most prevalent and powerful among the Baltic states, Poland, and a certain section of the Ukrainian population, many of whom see the Nazi and Soviet occupations as equivalent.[2] This gap of historical memory between two Europes has still not been overcome, and contributes to the divide over where Russia fits into Europe. However, these dividing lines have recently proven fluid, with some countries like Hungary and, to a lesser extent, Slovakia becoming more Russophile. Some European countries not yet members of the European Union, like Serbia and Montenegro, would potentially accentuate this Russophile group when they enter the European Union.

The European Union thus does not hold a unified view of the post-Soviet space: national memories remain important, in particular in shaping relations with Russia. Despite this diversity, EU institutions have succeeded in setting up two specific policies that target select post-Soviet countries: the Eastern Partnership and the Strategy for Central Asia.

THE EASTERN PARTNERSHIP

Throughout the 1990s, the European Union had very little presence in the South Caucasus; it maintained a single Commission Delegation for all three countries, which it opened in Tbilisi in 1995. Partnership and Cooperation Agreements (PCAs) with the individual states came into force only later, in 1999, and were less extensive than those concluded with Russia, Ukraine, and

---

1. See Jos Boonstra, "The South Caucasus and its Wider Neighbourhood" (working paper, n.p.: CASCADE, December 2015), http://www.cascade-caucasus.eu/wp-content/uploads/2015/09/Cascade-D8-Caucasus-Wider-Neighbourhood .pdf; and, by the same author, "The South Caucasus concert: Each playing its own tune" (working paper no. 128, n.p.: FRIDE, September 2015), http://www.cascade-caucasus.eu/wp-content/uploads/2015/09/WP-128-ok.pdf.

2. See the research project Memory at War: Cultural Dynamics in Poland, Russia and Ukraine (MAW), http://heranet .info/maw/index.

Moldova. The European view changed during the 2000s: with the arrival of new members such as Romania and Bulgaria, the Black Sea became one of the frontiers of the European Union. In 2003, the European Union created a position of a special representative for the South Caucasus. The Georgian Rose Revolution of December 2003 and the energy crises between Russia and the transit countries in 2005–2006, which confirmed the need to diversify energy supplies and transit routes, pushed the European Union to become more active in the region. Brussels's new model of cooperation, the European Neighbourhood Policy (ENP), covered both Eastern Europe, including South Caucasus, and the Middle East–North Africa (MENA) region. The ENP was later bifurcated, with the Union of the Mediterranean for MENA set up in 2008 and in 2009 the Eastern Partnership created for Eastern Europe.[3] The same year, the fruit of a joint initiative of Poland and Sweden, and in a context in which the European Union left strengthened from its mediation during the 2008 Russian-Georgian conflict, the European Union also proposed new association agreements to Armenia, Azerbaijan, Georgia, Moldova, Ukraine, and Belarus to replace the existing PCAs.[4]

The Eastern Partnership enables the six partner countries to strengthen their political, economic, and cultural ties with the European Union, allowing them to conclude deep and comprehensive free-trade agreements (DCFTAs). It also envisages the conclusion of pacts of mobility and security and the progressive liberalization of visa regimes, which ought eventually to enable the free movement of citizens of these countries within the Schengen zone. Thanks to this partnership, the European Union has individualized its relationships with each of the partner states, emphasizing bilateral rapprochement. The three South Caucasus countries are thus no longer treated by the European Union as a regional ensemble—but as partners with distinct expectations.[5]

The potential effects of the Eastern Partnerships for post-Soviet countries are nevertheless difficult to measure. The level of free trade foreseen by the agreement requires painful adaptations, including an alignment with the requisite community norms (the so-called *acquis communataire*, i.e., the principle of the supremacy of and direct effect of European law, acts issued by EU institutions, and all other acts adopted on the basis of constituent treaties), which are very financially and administratively costly. It also requires the partner country to commit to the European Union's fundamental values, meaning democracy, the rule of law, the respect for human rights, and fundamental freedoms.[6]

---

3. Jos Boonstra and Natalia Shapovalova, "The EU's Eastern Partnership: One year backwards" (working paper no. 99, n.p.: FRIDE, May 2010), http://fride.org/download/WP99_EP_ENG_may10.pdf.

4. For a history of EU–South Caucasus relationships, see Laure Delcour and Hubert Duhot, "Bringing South Caucasus Closer to Europe? Achievements and Challenges in ENP Implementation," College of Europe Natolin Research Paper no. 2011/3 (April 7, 2011), http://ssrn.com/abstract=1923753.

5. See European Commission High Representative of the Union for Foreign Affairs and Security Policy, *Review of the European Neighbourhood Policy* (November 18, 2015), 1–21, http://eeas.europa.eu/enp/documents/2015/151118_joint -communication_review-of-the-enp_en.pdf.

6. Jeanne Park, "The European Union's Eastern Partnership," Council on Foreign Relations, March 14, 2014, http://www .cfr.org/europe/european-unions-eastern-partnership/p32577.

Since its launch in 2009, the Eastern Partnership has had some successes and some failures. Two groups of countries eventually appeared, those who signed association agreements (Georgia, Moldova, Ukraine) and those who did not (Armenia, Azerbaijan, Belarus).

The European Union signed association agreements with both Georgia and Moldova in June 2014. Satisfactory progress was also made with Tbilisi and Chişinău on the path to bilateral trade liberalization and the implementation of agreements designed to relax visa regulations, and of readmission agreements. Ukraine ratified the association agreement on June 27, 2014, but at the cost of war with Russia, the annexation of Crimea and a protracted conflict in Donbas. The chapters dealing with political dialogue, legal issues, freedom and security, and economic, financial and sectoral cooperation came into force on a provisional basis on November 1, 2014, whereas the beginning of the extensive and complete free-trade zone was suspended until December 31, 2015. Although Ukrainian public opinion is now distinctly more pro-EU and pro-NATO than it was before the Russian crisis, the advance of the European Union at the price of a war and the weakening of the Ukrainian state is a stinging failure for European soft power.

This association approach failed, however, with regard to Armenia, Azerbaijan, and Armenia negotiated for an association agreement[7] but ultimately decided instead to join the Russian-led Eurasian Economic Union (EEU), which came into force on January 1, 2015. Although Armenia suspended its negotiations over an association agreement in July 2013, Yerevan and Brussels nevertheless began talks on relaxing visa regulations and readmission requirements, as well as on the possibility that Armenia might participate in some EU programs and agencies. Azerbaijan entered for a few months into negotiations on an association agreement in 2010, and cooperation is developing in the energy sector, but the deterioration of the domestic political situation and growing authoritarianism within the country have curbed any prospects of Baku concluding an agreement with the European Union any time soon.[8] Belarus never even entered into negotiations with a view to an EU association agreement.

STRATEGY FOR CENTRAL ASIA

In 2007, while the European Union was drawing up the Eastern Partnership policy, it also recognized the need for a better strategy toward Central Asia. Anticipated energy partnerships with Kazakhstan and Turkmenistan, energy wars with Russia, and China's then-burgeoning economic power encouraged the European Union to better structure its partnership with the region. EU member states were becoming increasingly present locally, among others, on the military level as part of International Security Assistance Force (ISAF) operations in Afghanistan (German forces operated out of a base in Termez, Uzbekistan, while the French air force used Dushanbe Airport in Tajikistan). In addition, Europe has finally become aware of its economic weight as one of the main

7. Iana Dreyer and Nicu Popescu, "A solidarity package for the eastern partners," European Union Institute for Security Studies, September 2013, http://eap-csf.eu/en/news-events/articles-analytics/a-solidarity-package-for-the-eastern-partners-by-iana-dreyer-and-nicu-popescu/.

8. European Parliament, "Fact Sheets on the European Union," September 2015, http://www.europarl.europa.eu/atyourservice/fr/displayFtu.html?ftuId=FTU_6.5.5.html.

trading partners of the Central Asian states, aiming to leverage member states' bilateral economic relations to enhance European influence in the region.[9]

Since the adoption of the Lisbon Treaty the same year, the commission's delegations abroad have been converted into the European Union Delegation—or offices—of the European External Action Service (EEAS), mandated to represent the totality of EU authorities.[10] EU missions operate in Kazakhstan, Kyrgyzstan, Tajikistan, and Uzbekistan, and in Turkmenistan, a Europa House is awaiting a status upgrade. The nomination, since 2005, of an EU special representative (EUSR) for Central Asia attests to the European Union's growing presence alongside the diplomatic representation of its member states. Officially, there is no friction between the EU representations and those of member states, but in some cases member states act independently of the European Union, for instance, Germany in negotiating agreements to secure its military basis in Termez, with little EU involvement.

In 2007, under the impetus of Germany, the driving force of European involvement in Central Asia, the European Union adopted a new strategy designed to reinforce its presence in the region. This new strategy represents an extension of European links with its Central Asian neighbors (and Russia), while also being a policy in its own right, one that makes use of separate funding mechanisms and structures. The main change brought by the new strategy is that the European Union has ceased considering Central Asia as a unified region, and has sought to take into account the diversity of national situations by allocating a large part of its aid according to each country's specific needs. For instance, based on estimates by the World Bank and the Organization for Economic Co-operation and Development (OECD), the European Union considers that, given its resources, Kazakhstan no longer requires direct financial support, except in specific sectors such as higher education and civil society, and the same will be true for Turkmenistan as of 2017. Kazakhstan continues nonetheless to be the most involved of the Central Asian countries with the European Union. Relations with Turkmenistan and Uzbekistan are limited by the authoritarian and isolationist approaches of both regimes. The European Union thus focuses its aid policy on the two most fragile states, Kyrgyzstan and Tajikistan, a logic reinforced by the review of European strategies undertaken in 2012 as well as in 2015.[11]

European aid is oriented around seven broad priorities: human rights, rule of law, good governance, and democratization; youth and education; economic development, trade, and investment; strengthening energy and transport links; environmental sustainability and water; combating common threats and challenges; and intercultural dialogue.[12] But the sum allocated to the region

9. Michael Emerson and Jos Boonstra, rapporteurs, *Into EurAsia: Monitoring the EU's Central Asia Strategy* (Brussels: Centre for European Policy Studies, 2010). Parts of this report on Central Asia rely on EUCAM (Europe–Central Asia Monitoring) research and publications.

10. See the official website of the European Union: http://eeas.europa.eu.

11. European Council, "Council conclusions on the EU Strategy for Central Asia," Brussels, June 22, 2015, http://www.consilium.europa.eu/en/press/press-releases/2015/06/22-fac-central-asia-conclusions/.

12. European Community, "Regional Strategy Paper for Assistance to Central Asia for the period 2007–2013," http://eeas.europa.eu/central_asia/rsp/07_13_en.pdf; European Community, "Central Asia Indicative Programme (2007–2010)," http://eeas.europa.eu/central_asia/rsp/nip_07_10_en.pdf.

by European bodies, which does not include the aid offered by member states, remains very modest: 750 million euros for the seven-year cycle 2007–2013, that is, about 20 million euros per country per year. The total for the new cycle 2014–2020 amounts to 1 billion euros. Of this amount, two-thirds is reserved for EU bilateral assistance toward poverty reduction and sustainable development, while the regional approach, which receives one-third of the assistance budget, is devoted solely to transnational questions such as tackling organized crime, drug trafficking, and water management.[13]

EU involvement in the Central Asian region is thus of a totally different magnitude and scope than that of the Eastern Partnership, which includes discussions on a free-visa regime, free trade and association agreements, and a certain normative convergence. Many EU initiatives had a limited impact. The democracy promotion, which is central to EU projection abroad, operates on rather difficult terrain in Central Asia. The Human Rights Dialogue process with each of the five Central Asian republics has had limited results, although there were some rare advances on prisoner rights, moratoriums on capital punishment, and the liberation of certain journalists.[14] The European Initiative for Democracy and Human Rights (EIDHR) funds the development of civil society and dialogue on human rights, but it could not hamper the closing of political space in the region.[15] EU regional initiatives are focused on water and environment,[16] education, and rule of law, to which should be added the already existing border management programs, Border Management Programme in Central Asia (BOMCA) and Central Asia Drug Action Programme (CADAP). Finally, the High-Level Security Dialogue, launched in 2012 with the hope to engage Central Asian countries in security discussions over Afghanistan, had to be canceled because of a lack of interest from the Central Asian side. Only EU initiatives in higher education and other cultural, soft-power tools seem able to meet with bigger and more lasting success in the region.

As summarized by Jos Boonstra, "Over the last eight years, the European Union has been successful in creating several institutionalized mechanisms for working and bolstering relations with Central Asian governments, including an increased presence on the ground. But the overall picture of the EU's engagement in Central Asia is one of limited to no impact."[17]

---

13. Neil Melvin and Jos Boonstra, "The EU Strategy for Central Asia @ Year One," *EUCAM Policy Brief* no. 1 (October 2008), http://fride.org/download/OP_The_EU_Strategy_ENG_oct08.pdf.

14. Katharina Hoffmann, "The EU in Central Asia: Successful good governance promotion?," *Third World Quarterly* 31, no. 1 (2010): 87–103.

15. Vera Axyonova, "Promoting Justice Reforms in Central Asia: The European Union's Rule of Law Initiative as Part of a Comprehensive Democratization Strategy?," *Central Asian Affairs* 3, no. 1 (2016): 29–48.

16. European Commission, "Central Asia—Environment," http://ec.europa.eu/europeaid/regions/central-asia/eus -development-cooperation-central-asia-environment_en (accessed May 27, 2012).

17. Jos Boonstra, "Reviewing the EU's approach to Central Asia," *EUCAM Policy Brief* no. 34 (February 2015), http:// www.eucentralasia.eu/fileadmin/user_upload/PDF/Policy_Briefs/EUCAM-PB-34-Reviewing-EU-policies-in-Central -Asia-EN.pdf.

02

The European Union's Foreign Economic and Security Policy

Geographical contiguity between Europe and Eurasia means that security must be a high priority for both Brussels and the European national capitals. But however acute the European perception of security issues in Eurasia can be, the European Union and its member states lack the capacity and the structures for proactive steps. The Ukrainian crisis confirmed the difficulties in finding solutions to conflicts in the region, even those close to European borders. Moreover, the ability of European institutions to deal with several immediate crises at the same time is limited. The current migration crisis and the Syrian war are keeping all the European leadership circles busy, thus diminishing involvement in Eurasian issues.

To this should be added Europe's difficulty, already mentioned above, to reach consensus about relations with Russia, and the need for either a more confrontational or, on the contrary, a more cooperative approach. Last but not least, the European Union's security-related tools are limited. The European Union's status as a hard-security actor on the international scene remains weak at best, and most European countries place their trust in NATO to guarantee their security on a global level. While the Common Security and Defense Policy (CSDP) runs several civilian and military missions around the world,[1] it remains hampered by internal divergences among member states on security and defense issues, by a lack of funding, and overlapping competencies with NATO. The European Union tends to focus on soft security through CSDP (Rule of Law missions, security service reform, border monitoring, and training), while NATO covers hard security. Ever since the Libyan crisis, the French intervention in Mali and its lack of support from countries like Germany, and the international coalition fighting the so-called Islamic State in Syria and Iraq, no specific European defense system separate from NATO has emerged.

The Eastern Partnership rests on the European Union's traditional approach in security matters, that is, on the strengthening of neighborhood links at all levels and rapprochement with European norms, but this soft-power strategy has had little effect on the ground in zones of conflict. Since

---

1. European Union External Action Service, "About CSDP—An Overview," http://eeas.europa.eu/csdp/about-csdp/index _en.htm.

2003 Brussels has deployed an EUSR for the South Caucasus and launched a European Security and Defense Policy (ESDP) mission there. Yet the European Union had little success and influence in the region, especially on the Nagorno-Karabakh conflict: it has no direct role in the peace talks, and its call for a peaceful settlement cannot genuinely influence either Baku or Yerevan, or even the elites of Stepanakert. As a cochair, France has been able to play a certain negotiating role, but not without some suspicion from the Azerbaijani side, given the large Armenian diaspora living in France. In the framework of its Instrument for Stability, Brussels launched a European Partnership for the Peaceful Settlement of the Conflict over Nagorno-Karabakh (EPNK), which, in theory, facilitates dialogue between civil society, media, and policymakers, for both conflicts.[2] However, the current revival of bellicose narratives on both sides, the growing military spending of Azerbaijan, and the inability to reconcile Turkey and Armenia shows that the impact of European policy is limited at best.

Europe was able to gain more visibility and sway during the Georgian conflict. EU and especially French mediation during the Russo-Georgian war of August 2008 helped contain the conflict and strengthened Brussels's influence in Tbilisi.[3] This mediation occurred outside the framework of the Eastern Partnership, but the European Union sent a border control mission to Georgia and the EUSR participated in the Geneva peace talks, two successes for Europe in its relationship to Tbilisi.

Central Asia offers a different picture. It has no open interstate conflicts, but instead faces several localized areas of tension in the Ferghana Valley; interethnic tensions in Kyrgyzstan; and regular riots between central forces and former warlords in some regions of Tajikistan such as the Rasht Valley and Gorno-Badakhshan. The June 2010 *Joint EU Council and Commission Implementation Report of the EU Strategy for Central Asia* recognizes the deficiencies of the 2007 Strategy in terms of security, and called for reinforced efforts in "security broadly speaking."[4] Its conclusion reads: "It will be necessary to expand the concept of security to include major international and regional challenges such as human security, the combating of drug trafficking and trafficking in human beings, precursors, nuclear and radioactive materials, uranium tailings, border management, bio-safety, bio-security, and the combating of terrorism and prevention of radicalization and extremism, including via a continued emphasis on poverty alleviation. Combating corruption is an important element in countering many of these security challenges."[5]

Yet prospects for a deeper EU security role in Central Asia remain limited. Central Asian governments are used to playing actors off against one another in order to get more financial support and technical assistance without having genuinely to commit to reform or transparency. They are not interested in giving any right of interference to any external player, especially one that has an

---

2. European Union, "The European Union continues to support civil society peace building efforts over Nagorno-Karabakh" (press release, November 6, 2012), http://www.consilium.europa.eu/uedocs/cms_data/docs/pressdata/en/foraff/133298.pdf.

3. Michel Foucher and Jean-Dominique Giuliani, "European Union and the Russo-Georgian War," *European Issues*, no. 108 (September 1, 2008), http://www.robert-schuman.eu/en/doc/questions-d-europe/qe-108-en.pdf.

4. European Council and European Commission, *Joint Progress Report by the Council and the European Commission to the European Council on the implementation of the EU Central Asia Strategy*, June 14, 2010, 6, http://register.consilium.europa.eu/doc/srv?l=EN&f=ST%2011402%202010%20INIT.

5. Ibid., 26.

agenda of accountability, or seeks some right to oversee the most opaque sector of their regimes, that is, the security services and the army. Though both the European Union and the local authorities share the same concerns about the possible rise of Islamist militancy, the gap between their respective definitions of what is creating insecurity and what the final goal of security aid is makes effective cooperation difficult.[6]

Moreover, European security assistance to Central Asia is often associated with institutions other than the European Union per se. The OSCE, for instance, has a border guard training program in Central Asia and a Border Management Staff College located in Dushanbe, while NATO has its own association strategies, via the Partnership for Peace (PfP) program, and an Individual Partnership Action Plan (IPAP) for Kazakhstan. Member states have also devised their own bilateral programs for training police or border guards. Many of these European-supported initiatives are limited to Kyrgyzstan and Tajikistan, the two weakest states in the region, and have difficulties moving from investing in hard infrastructure (new buildings, new equipment) toward genuine training in human capital. The best-known EU program for border securitization, BOMCA (Border Management Programme in Central Asia), long implemented by the United Nations Development Programme (UNDP), focuses on the upgrading and/or building of border posts, on equipping them with high-tech material, on training border guards for searching goods and people and detecting illicit substances, and on performing joint exercises with neighboring countries.[7] However, due to a lack of independent evaluation, it is unclear if any of these Western-led programs have had a positive impact, or if they are even sustainable. A similar issue is at stake with the European Union's counter-narcotics projects, which aim, on paper, at strengthening the Central Asian states' capacity to fight drug trafficking; these projects' effectiveness is quite limited given the role of many state structures in the trafficking itself.[8]

Only during the 2010 interethnic riots in southern Kyrgyzstan did the European Union become a critical external player in terms of security. The mediation offered to the Kyrgyz authorities by the EUSR at the time, Pierre Morel, reinforced Brussels's visibility and legitimacy in Bishkek. However, even in that case, the two Europe-led initiatives were virulently criticized by Kyrgyzstan. First, the Independent International Commission of Inquiry (KIC), which included members from Finland, Australia, Estonia, France, Russia, Turkey, and the United Kingdom, published a report in 2011 documenting serious violations of international law, infuriating the Kyrgyz government, which declared the commission's chair, Dr. Kimmo Kiljunen, persona non grata.[9] Second, the OSCE,

---

6. George Gavrilis, "The International Community's Elusive Search for Common Ground in Central Asia," PONARS Policy Memo 173 (May 2011), http://www.ponarseurasia.org/memo/international-communitys-elusive-search-common-ground-central-asia.

7. George Gavrilis, *Central Asia's Border Woes & the Impact of International Assistance*, Occasional Paper Series no. 6 (New York: Open Society Foundations, May 2012), https://www.opensocietyfoundations.org/sites/default/files/OPS-No-6-20120601.pdf.

8. Sebastien Peyrouse, "Drug Trafficking in Central Asia: A Poorly Considered Fight?," PONARS Policy Memo 173 (September 2012), http://www.ponarseurasia.org/memo/drug-trafficking-central-asia-poorly-considered-fight.

9. "Head of Commission on Kyrgyz Violence Declared Persona Non Grata," Radio Free Europe/Radio Liberty, May 26, 2011, http://www.rferl.org/content/head_of_commission_on_kyrgyz_violence_declared_persona_non_grata/24205930.html.

which planned to deploy 52 law-enforcement experts from OSCE member states to southern Kyrgyzstan, had to curtail its police mission after massive protests by the Kyrgyz political establishment.[10] Such difficulties in the most EU-friendly country of Central Asia demonstrate the obstacles facing EU security initiatives in the region.

RUSSIA

Unlike U.S. elites but similar to the Chinese elites, the European leadership has always acknowledged that Russia remains the dominant power in the Eurasian space, in the sense that it retains the strategic initiative and is the only country to be able to reverse the independence of its neighbors acquired in 1991 and undermine their sovereignty. The Ukrainian crisis gave it cause to continue to see the Eurasian space as largely molded by Russia. As mentioned, European perceptions of Russia diverge greatly between member states, their memories of the relationship with Russia, and depend on the individual ideological orientations of some EU constituencies.[11]

European institutions have always affirmed their support for projects promoting regional integration—which corresponds to one of the founding principles of the European construction— even if the power imbalance between Russia, on the one hand, and the smaller states, on the other, makes it difficult to compare the European Union with the Russian-backed Eurasian Economic Union. The European position on the Customs Union, and later on the Eurasian Economic Union, is therefore that regional integration is in principle positive, but only if it does not hamper joining the World Trade Organization (WTO) and if it maintains a balance between the various actors' legitimate interests. While Moldova and Georgia were able to sign association agreements without provoking a violent Russian reaction, Armenia was pushed to abandon its efforts at signing an association agreement and join the Eurasian Economic Union as, initially at least, was Ukraine. Nonetheless, the European Union remains Armenia's and Kazakhstan's main trade partner although both became EEU members.

Some voices in Europe propose that the European Union sign an agreement with the Eurasian Economic Union. On paper, the prospect of free trade between the European Union and the Eurasian Economic Union would simplify the situation of Ukraine, Moldova, and Georgia, and enhance global multilateral trade liberalization. However, some European elites and member states question the voluntary nature of EEU membership for some states, such as Kyrgyzstan and Armenia, the fact that some EEU members are not WTO members (Belarus), the use of unilateral trade protection measures by Russia, and the lack of will for integration shown by some members, if only in terms of the free movement of goods.[12] Russia's current economic crisis and the slowdown of EEU development, as well as the lack of will to pursue deeper integration, visible, among other

10. Natasha Yefimov, "OSCE Waters Down Police Mission to Kyrgyzstan," EurasiaNet.org, November 22, 2010, http://www.eurasianet.org/node/62421.

11. Marlene Laruelle, *Eurasianism and the European Far Right: Reshaping the Russia-Europe Relationship* (Lanham, MD: Lexington Books, 2015).

12. Nate Schenkkan, "Eurasian Disunion: Why the Union Might Not Survive 2015," *Foreign Affairs*, December 26, 2014, https://www.foreignaffairs.com/articles/armenia/2014-12-26/eurasian-disunion.

capitals, in Astana, could push the Eurasian Economic Union to become a relatively empty structure, limited to free trade cooperation, with no ability to shape the economic policies of its member states, which would allow the European Union to avoid having to recognize or cooperate with it.[13]

On security issues, Europe's position has always been straightforward. EU leaders and member states do not recognize the legitimacy of the Russia-led Collective Security Treaty Organization (CSTO), or seek to pursue cooperation with it. NATO continues to promote only country-to-country cooperation and does not accept the role that Moscow would like to see in the CSTO in shaping the military policy of its member states. That said, however, Europe's room for maneuver once again remains slight. Countries under Russian military influence such as Kazakhstan, Kyrgyzstan, Tajikistan, and Armenia have been winding down their military cooperation with Western countries since the mid-2000s. European militaries are less involved in Central Asia than in the past—the French military base in Tajikistan closed at the end of 2013[14] amid the withdrawal of French soldiers from Afghanistan, and Germany closed its Termez base at the end of 2015.[15] European military industries are also having more difficulty in penetrating the national defense markets of CSTO members, which can purchase Russian weapons at a discounted price.[16]

With some exceptions, such as the Baltic states, and to a lesser extent Poland and Romania, European countries argue that Europe cannot afford any conflict with Russia in their shared neighborhood. Europe has neither the financial nor the military capability to manage such a crisis in its Eastern Partnership zone, and even less in Central Asia, and is deeply involved in other financial or military theaters. European public opinion is focused on domestic socioeconomic issues and does not favor any engagement abroad, much less the creation of a new iron curtain in the name of solidarity with post-Soviet countries wanting to leave Russia's sphere of influence. The failure to prevent the Ukrainian conflict only worked to confirm that Europe is not ready to confront Russia except through economic sanctions. As the South Caucasus, and even more Central Asia, are farther away still from Europe, Russia's revival of influence in both regions will annoy European leaders, but this will not lead them to confront Russia head-on.

CHINA

For Brussels and the European capitals, the second external actor whose activities in Eurasia need monitoring, and to which European policy requires adapting, is China. At the institutional level, the European Union and the main China-led regional organization, the Shanghai Cooperation

13. Nicu Popescu, *Eurasian Union: The real, the imaginary and the likely*, Chaillot Papers 132 (Paris: EU Institute for Security Studies, September 2014), http://www.iss.europa.eu/uploads/media/CP_132.pdf.

14. Joshua Kucera, "French Military Begins Withdrawal from Tajikistan," EurasiaNet.org, May 5, 2013, http://www.eurasianet.org/node/66925.

15. Joshua Kucera, "Germany Says It's Closing Uzbekistan Air Base," EurasiaNet.org, October 15, 2015, http://www.eurasianet.org/node/75556.

16. "CSO Downgrades NATO Ties," Radio Free Europe/Radio Liberty, June 16, 2014, http://www.rferl.org/content/russia-led-csto-downgrades-nato-ties/25424241.html.

Organization (SCO), do not collaborate on any specific projects in Eurasia, though there have been some midlevel informal meetings. In principle the European Union is favorable to multilateral frameworks, especially if they focus on economic cooperation, and as such the SCO membership recently offered to India and Pakistan obviously attracts European attention. The European Union could potentially be interested in institutionalizing a partnership with the SCO on projects involving economic cooperation, or in having broad security-oriented discussions.[17] However, it remains to be seen if the SCO can develop into more than a superficial platform of coordination between its members, and be able to advance a genuine cooperation-based security agenda.

Europe essentially sees China's influence in Eurasia through the dual prism of its partnership with Russia and its role as the main economic engine for Central Asia. China's growing cooperation with Russia,[18] which comes at a time when the Europe-Russia relationship is deteriorating, may push Russia to act in a more confrontational manner, notably given its diminished interdependence with the West since the imposition of sanctions over the conflict in Ukraine. However, Russia has no interest in being too quickly "absorbed" into China's orbit either.[19] The almost hegemonic role China plays as an investor and trade partner in each of the five Central Asian republics[20] also shapes Brussels's approach to dealing with Beijing in the region. The fact that Turkmenistan replaced its dependency on Russian gas purchases with dependency on Chinese purchases is of concern to the European Union, which was hoping to get an agreement with Ashgabat on gas deliveries as part of the Southern Corridor project. China has emerged as the only alternative to Russian domination for Central Asian gas and oil exports: while Russia is trying to hamper every new European strategy to bypass it and connect Central Asian producers directly with European consumers, it seems unable to block the reorientation of flows toward China.

European leaders and experts have expressed their interest in China's "One Belt, One Road" initiative as well. They view it positively insofar as it will allow the Central Asian states to be better integrated into international trade and to get Chinese funding for big infrastructure projects, which no one else is ready to finance. However, many experts express concern about the lack of transparency of Chinese economic involvement in the region, as well as concerns related to work conditions, environmental issues, and general accountability. Competition between European and Chinese firms in Central Asia obviously plays in favor of the latter, since they are able to offer government-backed loans, which come without political conditionality and are cheaper.

---

17. Andy Yee, "Engaging Central Asia: The EU-Shanghai Cooperation Organisation (SCO) Axis," East Asia Forum, November 7, 2009, http://www.eastasiaforum.org/2009/11/07/engaging-central-asia-the-eu-shanghai-cooperation-organisation-sco-axis/.

18. Emma Graham-Harrison, Alec Luhn, Shaun Walker, Ami Sedghi, and Mark Rice-Oxley, "China and Russia: The World's New Superpower Axis?," The Guardian, July 7, 2015, http://www.theguardian.com/world/2015/jul/07/china-russia-superpower-axis.

19. Ivan Zuenko, "Connecting the Eurasian Economic Union and the Silk Road Economic Belt: Current Problems and Challenges for Russia," China in Central Asia (blog), October 30, 2015, http://chinaincentralasia.com/2015/10/30/connecting-the-eurasian-economic-union-and-the-silk-road-economic-belt-current-problems-and-challenges-for-russia/.

20. Raffaello Pantucci, "Looking West: China and Central Asia," China in Central Asia (blog), April 16, 2015, http://chinaincentralasia.com/2015/04/16/looking-west-china-and-central-asia/.

Nonetheless, some in Europe are interested in building more cooperative patterns between European and Chinese initiatives in the region, for instance, concerning rural development, where it would be possible to have complementary policies for training agricultural technical professionals, or concerning initiatives on poverty alleviation and the development of remote regions.[21] Cooperation with China could be based on a trade-off between European technical knowledge and Chinese funds and investments. Of course the European Union and European companies would need to assess on a case-by-case basis whether they would be simply transferring knowledge to China, with little gain either for themselves or for Central Asians.

More globally, many in Europe have also questioned the birth of a new continental route for Chinese goods to Europe: the project, and notably the launching of new express railway lines from Chinese maritime production centers to Europe's eastern borders through Kazakhstan and Russia, has not been coordinated with Europe at all. It could accelerate the arrival of Chinese products to Europe and jeopardize some local production.[22] The question here is thus China's global role as a world producer and the impact of its economic slowdown, more than its specific status in Eurasia.

THE UNITED STATES

The European Union and the United States have largely shared interests in Eurasia but go about them in different ways. The strongest commonalities include the pursuit of human-rights standards, democratic development, stability and security, and the broader economic and social development of the post-Soviet states. Naturally there are also divergences and differences.[23]

The United States and Europe are divided in their perception of the post-Soviet space as constituting a unified geopolitical region. While the U.S. Department of Defense and the National Security Council maintained Central Asia in their Eurasian portfolio, the U.S. State Department dissociated Central Asia from the post-Soviet space in 2005 by creating a Bureau for South and Central Asian Affairs, grouping the five Central Asian states with Afghanistan, Pakistan, India, Bangladesh, Bhutan, and Sri Lanka. Seen from Brussels, the U.S. decision makes no sense, and solely reflects the U.S. focus on reintegrating Afghanistan into the Central Asian region. The special representative for the European Union at the time, Pierre Morel, did not hesitate to talk of a "de-Europeanization" of Central Asia in the American vision, and complained that it would dissociate European and American policies by bringing South Asia into play, which is above all an American preserve. The U.S.-backed Turkmenistan-Afghanistan-Pakistan-India (TAPI) pipeline project has also been seen as diverging from European interests, as a South Asian

21. Sebastien Peyrouse, Jos Boonstra, and Marlène Laruelle, "Security and development in Central Asia: The EU compared to China and Russia" (working paper no. 11, n.p.: EUCAM, May 2012), http://www.eucentralasia.eu/fileadmin/user_upload/PDF/Working_Papers/WP11.pdf.

22. Sarah Lain, "Western Europe Is Missing the Boat on China's Silk Road," *Diplomat*, October 26, 2015, http://thediplomat.com/2015/10/western-europe-is-missing-the-boat-on-chinas-silk-road/.

23. Jos Boonstra and Marlène Laruelle, "EU-US Cooperation in Central Asia: Parallel Lines Meet in Infinity?," *EUCAM Policy Brief* no. 31 (July 2013), http://www.eucentralasia.eu/uploads/tx_icticontent/EUCAM-PB-31-EN-EU-US.pdf.

orientation for Turkmen gas potentially contradicts European hopes for Central Asian participation in the Southern Corridor.

This difference in perception can be explained by the fact that most U.S. policies concerning Central Asia have been directly linked to the war effort in Afghanistan, and therefore look "south," whereas Europeans see the region through the prism of its geographical proximity with Europe, and therefore look from a "west" perspective. Unlike the United States, the European Union's approach to Central Asia is fully separated from Afghanistan, and the progressive European withdrawal from this country did not give rise to new connectivity with the EU policy for Central Asia. The U.S. New Silk Road project found little resonance in European circles, for which it amounts to a grand narrative designed for Afghanistan's future, but which Brussels believes has no real ability to influence security and economic trends on the ground.

More concretely, EU and U.S. approaches to the South Caucasus and Central Asia often lack coordination or are undertaken without joint action. U.S. and EU bureaucratic traditions and budget cycles are largely divergent. Decisionmaking mechanisms in both Washington and Brussels are very complex, with a multitude of actors involved in each (State, Defense, White House and Congress for the former; the European Commission, Council, Parliaments and member states for the latter). Bilateral contact between U.S. assistant secretaries and EUSRs—at least twice a year—is not enough to consolidate coordination. European External Action Service desk officers only have ad hoc interaction with their American counterparts, and on the ground, EU delegation officials and U.S. embassy staff generally each go their own way.

Europeans and Americans meet regularly in the framework of NATO and the OSCE, and participate in different multilateral development assistance mechanisms, but delegating cooperation to transatlantic institutions is not enough to foster genuine cooperation. NATO is limited by internal divergences between European countries on actions to be taken in the Eurasian space; the OSCE is marginalized in a region where local governments are weary of democratization initiatives; and the UNDP is only one of many development actors, whereas the European Union and United States are scarcely able to make any decisive impact.

Obviously, the role of NATO has been revived by the Ukrainian crisis. In response to growing concerns of the eastern-flank countries, NATO and some individual allies had decided to step up their military presence in the Baltic states. This is mostly a U.S. initiative, seconded by Germany, the United Kingdom, and Denmark.[24] However, if the United States and the Europeans have been able to coordinate their response to the Ukrainian crisis and their positioning toward Russia, the leaked phone call by Victoria Nuland, U.S. assistant secretary of state, in which she says, "Fuck the EU," remains firm in European memory as a sign that the United States often dismisses European concerns and perceptions of their own neighborhood.[25] But with the transatlantic organizations' ambivalent role in Eurasia and the ongoing crisis in Ukraine, the European Union and the United

---

24. Frances Perraudin, "Britain to Station Troops in Baltic Region 'to Deter Russian Aggression,'" *The Guardian*, October 8, 2015, http://www.theguardian.com/uk-news/2015/oct/08/britain-station-troops-poland-latvia-lithuania-estonia-russian-aggression.

25. Ed Pilkington, "Angela Merkel: Victoria Nuland's remarks on EU are unacceptable," *The Guardian*, February 7, 2014, http://www.theguardian.com/world/2014/feb/07/angela-merkel-victoria-nuland-eu-unacceptable.

States would be well advised to build a carefully coordinated approach, most crucially in the fields of security, development, and values.

IRAN AND TURKEY

The European perspective on the roles of Iran and Turkey in Eurasia is seen through the prism of the Mediterranean Basin and the Middle East in general. In the contemporary European diplomatic culture and worldview, Iran and Turkey are critical countries for the conflicts in Syria and in Iraq, and their role here takes precedence over efforts to engage them elsewhere, including Eurasia.

For Europe, the key partner in its neighborhood is Turkey, a country that Brussels is following with some concern given its internal domestic evolutions—President Recep Tayyıp Erdoğan's growing authoritarianism, the revival of tensions over the Kurdish issue, and terrorist threats. EU-Turkey relations have changed dramatically over the last decade, and the prospects for Turkey's EU membership seem now linked to the broader situation in the Middle East. Ankara has secured its strategic autonomy and seeks to build for itself the role of a crossroads between Europe and the Middle East, a position that increases its status as a rising power but also opens the door for many potential instabilities, both domestically and regionally.[26] Turkey's ambiguous stance toward the Syrian conflict, the Islamic State, and the migration crisis monopolizes Europeans' attention, and its place in the Eurasian space has been largely downplayed, although it reemerged when Ankara positioned itself as a partner of Russia in energy matters. The proposed Turkish Stream pipeline, with an annual capacity of 63 billion cubic meters (bcm), first discussed between Russia's Gazprom and Turkey's BOTAŞ in December 2014, was designed to replace the canceled South Stream project.[27] If carried through, Turkish Stream would have allowed Russia to fully cut out Ukraine as a transit state while deepening the economic and energy connection with Turkey. However, the rapid and brutal deterioration of Russia-Turkey relations after the downing of a Russian warplane at the Turkish-Syrian border in November 2015 dramatically changed the regional landscape, with the rupture of the bilateral honeymoon and several retaliation measures by Moscow, including the cancellation of Turkish Stream.

As for Iran, its role in bridging Europe and southern Eurasia remains to be seen. The step-by-step reintegration of Tehran into the regional game, and the lifting of sanctions, which came into force in early 2016, opens up mouth-watering prospects for many European companies. Many stayed active in Iran right up to the hardening of sanctions and have woven many links, both direct and indirect (via the United Arab Emirates, for instance) with the country. It is possible that European companies establishing themselves in Iran in future years will seek to build up subsidiaries in Central Asia or in the Caucasus, or draw up regional strategies for southern Eurasia. However, it is

26. Demir Murat Seyrek and Amanda Paul, "Syrian Refugee Crisis: Turkey-EU Relations—The Return of Realpolitik?," *Parliament Magazine*, October 13, 2015, https://www.theparliamentmagazine.eu/blog/syrian-refugee-crisis-turkey-eu-relations-return-realpolitik.

27. Ilham Shaban, "Russia Starts Building 'Turkish Stream' Without Waiting for Turkey," *Russia Insider*, May 25, 2015, http://russia-insider.com/en/politics/russia-starts-building-turkish-stream-without-waiting-turkey/ri7363.

also probable that the magnet effect that the opening of the Iranian market is going to create will divert these companies from the—less attractive—markets of the South Caucasus and Central Asia.[28] On the strategic level, Kazakhstan's role will likely increase if it manages to set itself up as a mediator between Iran and the international community on the nuclear fuel bank issue, which could increase European focus on it in return.[29]

28. Sebastien Peyrouse, "Iran's Growing Role in Central Asia? Geopolitical, Economic and Political Profit and Loss Account," Al Jazeera, April 6, 2014, http://studies.aljazeera.net/en/dossiers/2014/04/2014416940377354.html.

29. Raushan Nurhsayeva, "Kazakhstan to Host IAEA Nuclear Fuel Bank to Assist Non-proliferation," Reuters, August 27, 2015, http://www.reuters.com/article/us-kazakhstan-nuclear-iaea-idUSKCN0QW0AO20150827.

03

The European Union in a Reconnecting Eurasia

Seen from Brussels and European capitals, the South Caucasus and Central Asia are part of three meta-geoeconomic regions: the European, the Russian, and the Chinese. The U.S. focus on Central Asia and South Asia is not considered relevant, and Brussels does not foresee for the medium term any rapid economic integration of Central Asia with South Asia. Moreover, the U.S. focus on South Asia does not leave any room for the South Caucasus, which has no prospect of being connected to India or Pakistan. Seen from Europe, Iran is not considered as an economic region per se but is usually grouped into the European geoeconomic region as a potential transit state for Central Asian energy to reach Turkey and then Europe itself.

As soon as the Soviet Union collapsed, European actors launched projects to reconnect the South Caucasus and Central Asia on an east-west axis. The TRACECA (Transport Corridor Europe-Caucasus Asia) project aimed to open up Central Asia and the South Caucasus by creating a vast transport and communication corridor. Endowed with a budget of 110 million euros between 1993 and 2002, it financed the modernization of the ports of Ilyichevsk (Ukraine), Poti and Batumi (Georgia), Turkmenbashi (Turkmenistan), Baku (Azerbaijan), and Aktau (Kazakhstan), as well as the Kungrad-Beineu-Aktau railway, and organized the boat-railway linkup on the trip from Varna (Bulgaria) to Batumi and Baku to Aktau.[1] TRACECA met several simultaneous goals: first, a reduction of the dependence of the South Caucasus and Central Asia on Russia; second, preventing Iran from becoming a hub of regional commerce; and third, bolstering Turkey's role as a strategic partner for Europe, as well as of its key intermediary role with the newly independent states.

European and American projects to strengthen domestic economic ties between the countries of Central Asia and the South Caucasus nonetheless broadly failed, due to the lack of political will around regional cooperation, to conflicts and tension between states in the region, and because some sections of these countries' economies compete with one another. Moreover, compared with the declared ambition of the task, the budgets proposed by the European Union (on average two million euros per project) were too limited. Last, and above all, the economic profitability of

---

1. EU Neighbourhood Info Centre, "EuroEast: TRACECA," http://www.enpi-info.eu/maineast.php?id=272&id_type=10.

Table 3.1. 2014 European Union Trade in Goods with CIS (In Millions of Euros)

Country	EU Imports	EU Exports	Balance	Total Trade
Armenia	276	714	438	990
Azerbaijan	13,159	3,482	−9,677	16,641
Belarus	3,429	7,464	4,035	10,893
Georgia	657	1,912	1,254	2,569
Kazakhstan	23,900	6,754	−17,146	30,654
Kyrgyz Republic	79	402	322	481
Moldova	1,159	2,354	1,195	3,514
Russia	181,844	103,296	−78,549	285,140
Tajikistan	61	216	155	277
Turkmenistan	816	1,155	339	1,971
Ukraine	13,761	17,143	3,382	30,903
Uzbekistan	235	1,575	1,340	1,810
Total	**239,376**	**146,467**	**−92,912**	**385,843**

Source: European Commission, http://ec.europa.eu/.

the route is questionable: not only does transport through Russia enable a major time gain, but the numerous taxes demanded by the excessive number of transit states through which this east-west trade has to pass, reduces the margins.[2]

EUROPEAN TRADE AND INVESTMENT

Though in many cases the European Union has become one of the major economic partners of post-Soviet countries, this economic presence does not necessarily translate into political influence. For starters, the European Union has no mandate to oversee the trade and investment policies of its member states. Second, since European economic advances are often generated

2. Evgeny Vinokurov, Murat Jadraliyev, and Yury Shcherbanin, *The EurAsEC Transport Corridors* (Almaty, Kazakhstan: Eurasian Development Bank, March 2009), 23, http://www.eabr.org/general/upload/docs/EurAsEC_Trans_Cor.pdf.

by private actors, European institutions do not have specific instruments to take advantage of these successes, or to use them for leverage. Thus, by contrast with the United States, for example, where companies involved in the region can lobby Congress for better diplomatic relations with their partnering country, in Europe it is difficult to measure the sway that private firms have in shaping decisionmaking processes. French defense firms such as Thales can play a critical role in shaping France's policy toward Kazakhstan, for instance, or German firms toward Turkmenistan, but the causality of the relationship remains difficult to demonstrate, especially at the EU-wide level.

Bilateral economic cooperation is institutionalized through PCAs,[3] which are designed to guide post-Soviet countries on their transition to market economies, stimulate trade and investment, and push these countries to join the WTO and extend tariff preferences to each other under the Generalized System of Preferences (GSP).[4] Post-Soviet countries that are not WTO members—as of 2015, these include Turkmenistan, Uzbekistan, and Azerbaijan—are unable to access some EU trade preference mechanisms.

With the exceptions of countries that signed association agreements, the PCA remains the main legal framework for economic cooperation. PCAs do not include tariff preferences, but instead prohibit quantitative restrictions in bilateral trade and envisage, in select areas, the regulatory approximation of legislation to EU standards. In Kazakhstan, Kyrgyzstan, and Uzbekistan, PCAs entered into force after ratification in 1999, but Uzbekistan's PCA was suspended in 2005 after the Andijon events, only to be resumed in 2008.[5] The PCA with Tajikistan was signed in 2004 and ratified only five years later, in 2009; the PCA with Turkmenistan was signed in 1999, but two countries (the United Kingdom and France) still refuse to ratify it, as does the European Parliament.[6] Kazakhstan's PCA expired in 2009 and was continued by an enhanced PCA in 2013, confirming Kazakhstan's distinct status in Central Asia (see below). As an upper-middle-income-level economy, Astana has not been able to benefit from the GSP scheme since January 2014.

In practice, PCA objectives have not been always reached, and these general frameworks of cooperation have progressed with difficulty. The PCA legal framework does not, for instance, resolve the main issue impeding economic cooperation between Europe and the states of the South Caucasus and Central Asia, namely, the fact that many European companies are not attracted by the prospect of investing in Eurasia. The majority of post-Soviet countries remain difficult places to invest, despite some improvements in recent years. Some have established solid institutional frameworks for a market economy, such as Georgia, or to a lesser extent Ukraine, Kazakhstan, and Armenia; others have largely retained their state-owned economies as well as price and trade restrictions for many goods, especially Belarus, Turkmenistan, and Uzbekistan.

---

3. Emerson and Boonstra, *Into EurAsia*, 58.

4. European Council and Commission, "Partnership and Cooperation Agreements (PCAs): Russia, Eastern Europe, the Southern Caucasus and Central Asia," http://europa.eu/legislation_summaries/external_relations/relations_with_third _countries/eastern_europe_and_central_asia/r17002_en.htm (accessed May 31, 2012).

5. Emerson and Boonstra, *Into EurAsia*, 58.

6. Ibid. See also "Turkmenistan: Human Rights Prerequisite for Closer EU Ties," *Eurasia Review*, April 20, 2011, *http:// www.eurasiareview.com/20042011-turkmenistan-human-rights-prerequisite-for-closer-eu-ties/*.

European firms complain that they do not feel backed by their own governments and that they ought not to bear all the financial and political risks of investing in the region, which puts them at a disadvantage relative to their Russian or Chinese competitors. Moreover, European firms can only target strictly defined sectors of the local economies, often in rather sophisticated sectors that require know-how and high-tech capabilities, since lower-end niches—retail trade, the construction sector—have already been captured by far more competitive Chinese and to a lesser extent by Turkish firms.[7]

European economic policy in Eurasia can be dissociated by region or country. Ukraine constitutes a specific case, in particular since the crisis of 2014. Pending the entry into force of the DCFTA, the European Union is granting Ukrainian exporters continued preferential access to EU markets. The European Union committed 11 billion euros to help with Ukraine's economic and financial stabilization and reforms, including specific help for the regions worst hit by the crisis with Russia. The European Union is consequently the biggest international donor to Ukraine.[8]

Moldova along with the three countries of the Caucasus constitute a second category. The European Union is the main trading partner for all four, accounting for 46 percent of Moldova's total trade, around 40 percent of Azerbaijan's, 30 percent of Armenia's—but the latter's trade with EEU members is growing—and 26 percent of Georgia's.[9] For all four, EU exports are dominated by machinery, appliances, and transport equipment, as well as miscellaneous manufactured articles, manufactured goods, and chemicals. EU imports from Azerbaijan chiefly consist of mineral fuels, and for all the others of machinery and transport equipment, chemicals and agricultural products (food and live animals, beverages and tobacco).

In the Caucasus, the European Union had to face a growing diversification of trade paths. As Fiona Hill et al. note, "The differences between Armenia, Azerbaijan, and Georgia have become more definitive than the commonalities in their challenges, outlooks, and interests."[10] The landlocked character of Armenia—about two-thirds of its trade has to go through Georgia to reach Russia—at a time when Tbilisi and Yerevan have adopted increasingly divergent economic strategies is a good illustration of the difficulties involved for trade partners in developing any genuine long-term engagement in the region. Georgia's implementation of the EU tariff barriers will, for instance, create a kind of blockage over Armenian-Russian bilateral trade. Obstacles to developing European trade with the region are therefore both of a political—distrust between the three states, diverging geopolitical orientations, territorial disputes—and of an economic nature—lack of opportunities for European firms, and unfriendly business environments in Armenia and Azerbaijan.

---

7. Sebastien Peyrouse, "Business and Trade Relationship between the EU and Central Asia" (working paper no. 1, n.p.: EUCAM, June 2009), http://www.eucentralasia.eu/fileadmin/user_upload/PDF/Working_Papers/WP-No.1.pdf.

8. European Commission, "How the EU is supporting Ukraine" (fact sheet, May 22, 2015), http://europa.eu/rapid/press -release_MEMO-15-5035_en.htm.

9. European Commission Directorate-General for Trade, "Countries and Regions," http://ec.europa.eu/trade/policy /countries-and-regions/.

10. Fiona Hill, Kemal Kirişci, and Andrew Moffatt, *Retracing the Caucasian Circle: Considerations and Constraints for U.S., EU, and Turkish Engagement in the South Caucasus* (Washington, DC: Brookings Institution, July 2015), 4, http://www.brookings.edu/~/media/Research/Files/Reports/2015/07/south-caucasus-engagement/south_caucasus .pdf?la=en.

EU trade with Central Asia has grown, and the European Union is now one of the region's main trading partners, accounting for about a third of its overall external trade, on a par—depending on the country—with China and Russia. Central Asian exports to the European Union remain concentrated in a few commodities, especially crude oil from Kazakhstan and, to a lesser extent, from Turkmenistan and Uzbekistan; gas from Turkmenistan but also, though to a lesser extent, from Kazakhstan and Uzbekistan; and metals and cotton fibers. EU exports are dominated by machinery and transport equipment, and other manufactured goods.[11]

Since the beginning of the 1990s, Kazakhstan has emerged as Europe's principal Central Asian partner, with bilateral trade rising exponentially from $6.2 billion in 2003 (about 5.7 billion euros as of the time of this writing) to more than 30 billion euros in 2014.[12] Uzbekistan follows far behind in second place, while Turkmenistan is in third place. Trade with Kyrgyzstan and Tajikistan remains minuscule, and the presence of European companies in these two countries is still very limited and often linked to EU assistance programs. The European Union has become Kazakhstan's leading trade partner, with an almost 40 percent share in its total external trade, and its main foreign investor—with about half of Kazakhstan's foreign direct investment originating from the European Union—ahead of China and Russia. Among EU states, Germany is far in the lead, followed by a second tier comprising Italy, France, the Netherlands, and the United Kingdom. Kazakhstan is the European Union's third-largest trade partner in the former Soviet Union, after Russia and Ukraine, and José Manuel Barroso's visit to Astana in 2013—the first ever to the country by a president of the European Commission—confirmed the country's distinct status in the Central Asian region.[13]

ENERGY

Energy forms an important part of the EU relationship with the Eurasian region. The European Union needs to import 53 percent of all the energy it consumes (90 percent of its crude oil, 66 percent of its natural gas, 42 percent of its coal and other solid fuels, and 40 percent of its uranium and other nuclear fuels).[14] In 2014 it launched an EU Energy Security Strategy that promotes increasing energy efficiency as well as indigenous energy production, and aims to complete missing infrastructure links so that during a crisis energy can be redirected to where it is needed. This energy efficiency policy, as well as the EU climate policy, invites member states to diminish their carbon dioxide emissions by reducing oil and coal consumption, meaning that natural gas is likely to occupy a growing share of their energy mix, along with nuclear energy and renewables. Shale discoveries and fracking technologies are also revolutionizing the way the European Union

---

11. European Commission Directorate-General for Trade, "Countries and regions: Central Asia," http://ec.europa.eu /trade/policy/countries-and-regions/regions/central-asia/.

12. Directorate-General for Trade, *Kazakhstan* (report, Brussels: European Commission, 2015).

13. Niklas Norling, "Kazakhstan's Deepening Ties with Europe," *Central Asia-Caucasus Analyst*, November 11, 2014, http://www.cacianalyst.org/publications/analytical-articles/item/13091-kazakhstans-deepening-ties-with-europe.html.

14. European Commission, "Energy: Imports and secure supplies," https://ec.europa.eu/energy/en/topics/imports-and -secure-supplies.

Figure 1. Europe's Dependence on Russian Natural Gas Supplies

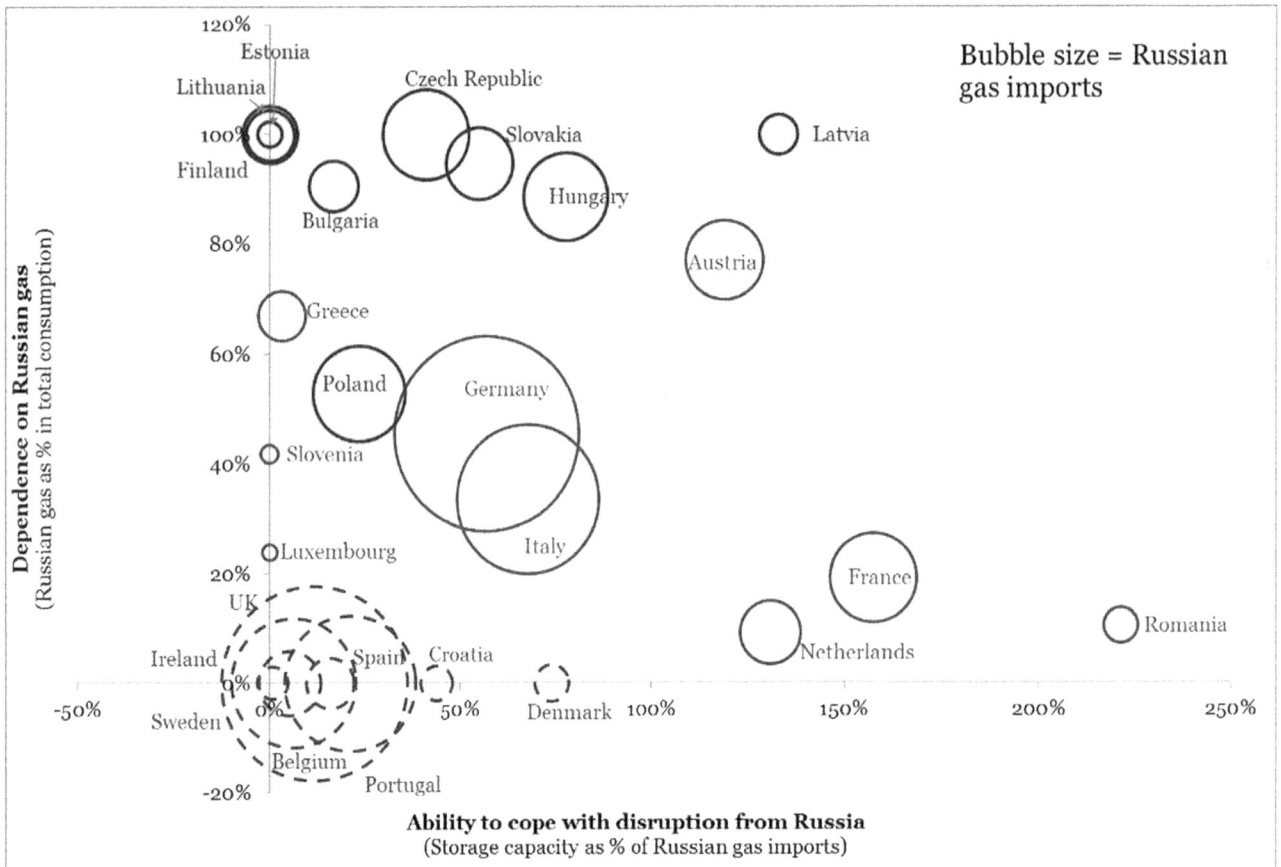

Source: IEA 2014 Natural Gas Information, http://www.ecfr.eu/article/commentary_europes_vulnerability _on_russian_gas.

Note: Due to lack of information, Malta and Cyprus have been excluded from the figures. These two coun- tries consume little gas and certainly receive no gas from Russia.

can develop a medium-term strategy for securing more independence from its traditional suppliers.

These prospects dramatically affect Russia, whose status as a gas superpower is now challenged, but also the whole of Eurasia.[15] However, dependence on Russian gas remains a critical issue for EU institutions and some member states. The three Baltic states and Finland import their entire natural gas consumption from Russia, either directly or through Belarus. The countries of Central Europe (Poland, Hungary, the Czech Republic, and Slovakia), as well as Bulgaria, are also very exposed to energy supply disruptions from Russia. Others are dependent on other, non-Russian sources, or else are almost self-sufficient, such as Romania (see Figure 1).

Despite the importance of ensuring secure access to energy, which impacts Europe's geopolitical autonomy, the European Union has yet to display complete unity over energy relations with Russia. The national strategy of each member state prevails over a united EU policy. Even the Third

15. William Courtney, Richard Kauzlarich, and Kenneth Yalowitz, "Can Eurasian Energy Compete?," *National Interest*, January 14, 2015, http://nationalinterest.org/feature/can-eurasian-energy-compete-12032.

Energy Package, signed in 2007 and outlining a set of rules unifying the European gas and electricity markets, has not been sufficient to overcome diverging national strategies, although Russia feels threatened by it and even opened a case against it at the WTO.[16] Russia has been able to strengthen its role as an energy supplier through new pipelines such as Nord Stream and the planned Turkish Stream, both of which bypass (or plan to) transit states, especially Ukraine. EU counterprojects have only partly succeeded in reinforcing energy cooperation with the other Eurasian states.

In the early 1990s the European Union financed the INOGATE (Interstate Oil and Gas Transportation to Europe) project, which covered the domains of oil and gas, electricity, renewable energy, and energy efficiency. It evolved into a broader energy partnership between the European Union and countries of the former Soviet Union, supplying technical studies on feasibility, institutional and legal support, and support for small-scale investments in interstate infrastructure, but it has shown few concrete results.[17] The launching, in 2005, of the Baku-Tbilisi-Ceyhan (BTC) oil pipeline from the Azeri-Chirag-Guneshli oil field in the Caspian Sea to the Mediterranean Sea has been seen as the first energy-related geopolitical success for both the United States and Europe.

The BTC pipeline, which helped solidify Baku's identification with the West, created an opportunity that the United States and European Union would like to seize to draw Kazakhstan into supplying oil and gas to Europe. Kazakh authorities, concerned about incurring Moscow's displeasure, had long been hesitant in making a clear commitment in favor of the BTC. In 2006, the Caspian Oil Transport System, an intergovernmental agreement between Azerbaijan and Kazakhstan, committed Astana to exporting oil via the BTC. Kazakhstan began developing new infrastructure, the Kazakhstan Caspian Transportation System (KCTS), along its Caspian shore, linking Atyrau and Aktau in order to export Caspian oil by sea and reach the Sangachal Terminal in Azerbaijan by tanker, with a capacity of 500,000 barrels per day (79,000 m^3/d) in the initial stage, later rising up, at least on paper, to 1.2 million barrels per day (190×10^3 m^3/d). However, mostly due to the postponement of the second phase of the Kashagan field's development until at least 2018, the KCTS project has been put on hold.[18] Turkmenistan has also joined the pipeline: since 2010, Ashgabat's purchase of three tankers from Russia has made it possible to transport about 40,000 barrels per day to Baku. However, no long-term solutions have been drawn up.

Europe-Eurasia gas cooperation has been more challenging. In 2006 the Baku-Tbilisi-Erzerum (BTE) gas pipeline was launched, transporting Azeri gas from the BP-operated offshore site of Shah Deniz to Turkey. The European Union then got very involved in promoting a Southern Gas Corridor that would allow it to diversify its supplies by bringing in gas from the Caspian countries, the Middle East, and the Eastern Mediterranean Basin. The Southern Corridor as defined by the European Commission consists of several gas pipeline projects, many which have thus far failed to materialize. The main accomplishment thus far has been the launching in 2015 of the

16. Yury Maltsev, "Russia sues EU over 'Third Energy Package'—Report," *Russia Today*, April 30, 2014, https://www.rt.com/business/156028-russia-sues-eu-energy/.

17. Emerson and Boonstra, *Into EurAsia*, 77–78.

18. Elena Kosolapova, "No Progress Expected in Kazakhstan's Caspian Oil Transportation System," Trend News Agency, October 22, 2014, http://en.trend.az/casia/kazakhstan/2324956.html.

Trans-Anatolian Natural Gas Pipeline (TANAP). Jointly owned by Azerbaijan, Turkey, and BP, TANAP should begin delivering Azerbaijani gas to Turkey, and then to the Balkans and Italy, as early as 2018. Its planned capacity would go from 16 billion cubic meters (bcm) at an early stage to 31 bcm in ten years, and potentially to 60 bcm if Turkmen gas can reach it and complement Azerbaijani.[19] TANAP will connect to TAP, the Trans-Adriatic Pipeline, which will bring the gas through Greece and Albania and then to Italy.

In the years to come, Azerbaijani gas will have to be supplemented with new sources, either from the Middle East or from Central Asia. If the Southern Corridor has been successful in delivering Azerbaijani gas to Europe, the place of Central Asia in it has been marginal to date. For Central Asian gas to reach Azerbaijan, several options have been discussed. The main one, which emerged in the early 1990s, is the project for a Trans-Caspian gas pipeline, one that never left the drawing board. The difficulties are simultaneously legal (the status of the Caspian Sea is still not settled, so agreement among all five littoral states would be necessary to build a pipeline); technical (shallow water, unstable climate, frequent storms, and environmental risks); and geopolitical (Russia and Iran are blocking the development of east-west axes). Another option, transporting Kazakh and Turkmen gas as liquefied natural gas (LNG), by tanker across the Caspian, would necessitate huge investments in infrastructure, which are not presently attracting investors.[20]

In the European Southern Corridor strategy, Turkmenistan has been as a key piece. Turkmen gas could come from the offshore deposit of Serdar-Kyapaz, which would cost only a modest amount to link up to the export network at Shah Deniz but would require that the territorial conflicts between Ashgabat and Baku be settled. Gas could also come from the onshore South Yolotan–Osman deposit, in which case the linking costs would be far greater. For this project to be realized, the European Union and Turkmenistan would have first to come to an understanding on prices and then to withstand Russian and Iranian, and possibly Chinese, pressures. Moreover, Brussels would have to negotiate with the Extractive Industry Transparency Initiative, which makes provision for more transparency in the management of resources by producer countries, as Turkmenistan is classified as one of the most opaque countries in the world.[21] Since the end of the 2000s, the European Union and Turkmenistan have repeatedly stated their commitment to energy cooperation, but without any precise agreement. Since then Beijing has emerged as Turkmenistan's near monopsonistic buyer—about 80 percent of Turkmen gas exports are now directed toward China. If the Turkmen authorities want to avoid total dependency on China, they will have to reopen discussions with Europe, but such a push does not appear likely to come either from Ashgabat or from Brussels in the short term.

19. Trans Anatolian Natural Gas Pipeline Project, "Why TANAP?," http://www.tanap.com/tanap-project/why-tanap/.

20. Nazyk Muradova. "An Ideal Investor to Come: Diversification of the Energy Exports of Turkmenistan," Central Asia Fellowship Papers no. 10 (George Washington University, August 2015), http://centralasiaprogram.org/blog/2015/08/24/an-ideal-investor-to-come-diversification-of-the-energy-exports-of-turkmenistan/.

21. Sebastien Peyrouse, *Turkmenistan: Strategies of Power, Dilemmas of Development* (Armonk, NY: M. E. Sharpe, 2011); Vanessa Boas, *Energy and Human Rights: Two Irreconcilable Foreign Policy Goals? The Case of the Trans-Caspian Pipeline in EU-Turkmen Relations*, IAI Working Papers, no. 12/07 (Rome: Instituto Affari Internazionali, March 2012), http://www.iai.it/en/pubblicazioni/energy-and-human-rights-two-irreconcilable-foreign-policy-goals.

As of now, the Middle East and the Eastern Mediterranean Basin seem to be better positioned to deliver gas to Europe than the Central Asian countries. The importance of Central Asia concerning energy for Europe, often highlighted in European discourses, must therefore be questioned, and seems to be mostly a statement of intent, intended to offer an easy and consensual narrative about shared interests.

04

Conclusion

Europe's influence in shaping the security and economic landscape of Eurasia operates through multiple channels, and is destined to remain fragmented. European policies toward Ukraine, the countries of the Eastern Partnership, and Central Asia will come to share fewer and fewer features. This is why Europe's strategy in helping Ukraine become a stable and functional country is so critical: much of Europe's long-term influence throughout Eurasia will be judged in the light of its success or failure in Ukraine. In the near and medium-term future, Europe's presence in the South Caucasus will be increasingly challenged by the divergence of trajectories of the three countries, which necessitates that Brussels develop more individualized projects for cooperation. Renewed risks of war in Nagorno-Karabakh or in Georgia's secessionist regions would also be read by neighboring countries as Europe's partial failure to become attractive enough to be able to influence the decisionmaking in these countries. In Central Asia, European involvement is bound to remain limited, and Europe will find it difficult to compete against the influence of Russia and China. The European posture toward both actors is still largely undefined: room for cooperation with China in Central Asia is inherently limited, while many European actors are wary of pursuing cooperative strategies with Russia, especially in the security sector—the more so after the crisis in Ukraine.

Moreover, EU structures have been weakened by the divergent positions of member states toward Russia's role in Eurasia, both in terms of energy policy and since the Ukrainian crisis. The European Union should find a way to cumulate and take advantage of its member states' individual roles, not necessarily try to unify them. Not only some of the member states themselves but also many private companies do not automatically support the European Union's value-oriented narrative. On the other side, European civil society has virulently criticized the conciliatory policies of the European Commission and its representatives on Central Asian affairs. European policy also lacks a more structured coordination with that of the United States, and only NATO and the OSCE appear to embody unified trans-Atlantic interests. The ability of Europe and Turkey to cooperate in Eurasia has also suffered setbacks in recent years, diminishing further the European Union's influence in Eurasia. However, Europe's influence is largely based on its soft power of attraction—the example of its own well-being, quality of life, educational opportunities, know-how, and technologies. Europe's legitimacy on these points is suffering at present on account of the economic slowdown, the debt crisis, and the inability to offer a solution to the migrant crisis. Europe's own path of development is viewed with mounting skepticism among a growing segment of public opinion in post-Soviet countries, while both the Russian narrative, as well as Islamist propaganda in some places, are helping to discredit the European model and liberal values more broadly. These factors combine to reduce Europe's capacity to promote good governance, and impact its ability to shape the economic and security future of many countries of Eurasia.

About the Author

Marlene Laruelle is research professor of international affairs and associate director of the Institute for European, Russian, and Eurasian Studies (IERES) at the Elliott School of International Affairs, George Washington University. She is a member of the Brussels-based EUCAM (Europe–Central Asia Monitoring), and she was a visiting scholar at the Woodrow Wilson International Center for Scholars (2005–2006). She holds a Ph.D. from the National Institute for Oriental Languages and Cultures in Paris. She is the coauthor of *Globalizing Central Asia: Geopolitics and the Challenges of Economic Development* (M. E. Sharpe, 2013) and *The "Chinese Question" in Central Asia: Domestic Order, Social Change, and the Chinese Factor* (Columbia University Press, 2012) and the editor of *China and India in Central Asia: A New "Great Game"?* (Palgrave Macmillan, 2010) and *Eurasianism and the European Far Right* (Lexington, 2015).